T0413421

Snakes

Slither and Hiss

FIRST EDITION
Series Editor Deborah Lock; **US Editor** John Searcy; **Art Editor** Mary Sandberg;
Production Editor Siu Chan; **Production** Pip Insley; **Jacket Designer** Martin Wilson;
Reading Consultant Linda Gambrell, PhD

THIS EDITION
Editorial Management by Oriel Square
Produced for DK by WonderLab Group LLC
Jennifer Emmett, Erica Green, Kate Hale, *Founders*

Editors Grace Hill Smith, Libby Romero, Michaela Weglinski;
Photography Editors Kelley Miller, Annette Kiesow, Nicole DiMella; **Managing Editor** Rachel Houghton;
Designers Project Design Company; **Researcher** Michelle Harris; **Copy Editor** Lori Merritt;
Indexer Connie Binder; **Proofreader** Larry Shea; **Reading Specialist** Dr. Jennifer Albro;
Curriculum Specialist Elaine Larson

Published in the United States by DK Publishing
1745 Broadway, 20th Floor, New York, NY 10019

Copyright © 2023 Dorling Kindersley Limited
DK, a Division of Penguin Random House LLC
24 25 26 27 10 9 8 7 6 5 4 3 2
003–333437–Apr/2023

All rights reserved.
Without limiting the rights under the copyright reserved
above, no part of this publication may be reproduced, stored
in or introduced into a retrieval system, or transmitted, in any
form, or by any means (electronic, mechanical, photocopying,
recording, or otherwise), without the prior written permission
of the copyright owner.
Published in Great Britain by Dorling Kindersley Limited

A catalog record for this book
is available from the Library of Congress.
HC ISBN: 978-0-7440-6710-1
PB ISBN: 978-0-7440-6711-8

DK books are available at special discounts when purchased
in bulk for sales promotions, premiums, fundraising, or
educational use. For details, contact: DK Publishing Special Markets,
1745 Broadway, 20th Floor, New York, NY 10019
SpecialSales@dk.com

Printed and bound in China

The publisher would like to thank the following for their kind permission to reproduce their images:
a=above; c=center; b=below; l=left; r=right; t=top; b/g=background

naturepl.com: Daniel Heuclin 26-27; **Shutterstock.com:** Patrick K. Campbell 12, 32bl, Joe McDonald 12-13

Cover images: *Front:* **Dreamstime.com:** Narupon Nimpaiboon (viper); **Shutterstock.com:** Astira 99;
Back: **Dreamstime.com:** Ondej Prosick cla; **Shutterstock.com:** Maureen Kirk cra

All other images © Dorling Kindersley

For the curious
www.dk.com

Level

2

Snakes

Slither and Hiss

Fiona Lock

Contents

Snakes in Action

Scaly Snakes

See the scaly snakes slither
here and there.

Slither!

scales

Rat Snakes

This baby rat snake slides out of its egg.

egg

Hiss!

Copperheads

This copperhead flicks its
tongue in and out.
It uses deadly venom
when it bites.

tongue

Parrot Snakes

This parrot snake opens its jaws wider and wider. It eats lizards and frogs.

Hiss!

jaws

Pit Vipers

This pit viper bites with its sharp fangs.
It has pit organs on its face to sense prey.

pit
organ

fangs

Rattlesnakes

Do you hear that
rattling sound?
This rattlesnake
rattles its tail when
it is angry.

Rattle!

tail

Cobras

This cobra is getting
ready to spit.
It aims for the eyes!

Ssspit!

hood

Pythons

This python wraps
around a rat and
squeezes tight.
It keeps squeezing until
the rat stops moving.

Sssqueeze

rat

Snakes All Around

Gaboon Vipers

This Gaboon viper hides in the leaves. It does this using camouflage.

leaves

Ssssh!

snake

Sea Snakes

This sea snake swims
this way and that.
It cannot move on land.

stripes

Ssswish!

Flying Tree Snakes

Look up in the trees!
This flying tree snake
glides from branch
to branch.

body

branch

Sleeping Snakes

See the sleepy snakes curl up in coils.

coil

Ssssh!

Can you slither
and hiss like a snake?

Glossary

Camouflage
[KAM-uh-flahj]
A way for animals to disguise their appearance to blend in with their surroundings

Egg
A soft, leathery shell with a baby snake growing inside

Fang
A large, hollow tooth that shoots out venom

Jaws
Bones that open and close the mouth

Pit Organs
Special sensors found in pits between their eyes and noses that allow pit vipers to sense heat from their prey

Scales
Small, smooth plates that cover the skin

Tongue
A mouth part that can smell, touch, and taste

Venom
A deadly chemical that some snakes inject into their prey by biting them

Index

Quiz

Answer the questions to see what you have learned. Check your answers in the key below.

Which snake am I?

1. I can open my jaws wide, and I eat lizards and frogs.

2. I bite with sharp fangs, and I have pit organs on my face.

3. I rattle my tail when I am angry.

4. I can hide in leaves using camouflage.

5. I can glide through the air from one tree branch to another.

1. A parrot snake 2. A pit viper 3. A rattlesnake
4. A Gaboon viper 5. A flying tree snake